Praise for ***Beastie, Baby and the Brai***

Trauma and dissociation are so little understood in the world in which we [illegible] ur child begins to have 'behaviour issues' that regular parenting strategies seem to have no impact upon, meltdowns which appear to have no real trigger and 'mood swings' that make it seem like you have two (or more!) children in one, you seek help; you need answers. When you first hear your child has developmental trauma and that your child is dissociating to survive that trauma, you are catapulted into a whole new realm with a new language and new rules of its own. It is so hard to understand and to get your head around it all. To date, there has been so little material that explains what's happening in terms that can be easily understood.

What Jess has done in writing about Dolly, helps to explain the 'behaviour issues', 'mood swings', and the apparently different children in one body. It is so important to have this understanding so you can begin to understand your child and help them to understand themselves. In doing so, you encourage your child to get to know their parts and help them to feel safe, understood and accepted just as they are.

Jess' book models how to begin to understand, accept and embrace your child's dissociative parts and how to deal with the behaviours each presents in a way that does not shame, therefore perpetuating the trauma, but instead brings acceptance, healing and wholeness.

Gaynor Foxley, Behaviour Support Specialist / Specialist Teacher

Having read this book for children, I think it is an absolutely fantastic resource. I can think of so many children I have worked with who would benefit from reading it with a caregiver. I also believe that it will help adults to use the scripts and language from the book and support them to develop their approaches when working or living with a child who dissociates.

This is an absolutely fantastic read and extremely insightful.

Rachael Gartland, Specialist Paediatric Occupational Therapy Ltd, Sensory Attachment Therapist, Sensory Integration Practitioner

Beastie Baby and the Brand-New Daddy explains and makes sense of dissociation in a way that everyone can understand. Tools and techniques to help this group of children are seamlessly interwoven into the story and can be adapted and applied in a variety of settings. A brilliant resource!

Danny Calmels, Pastoral Support Manager, Robert Bloomfield Academy

The survival response of dissociation is so often misunderstood or overlooked in children who have experienced trauma.

This engaging and accessible book is a valuable resource for anyone supporting or caring for a child who dissociates to manage overwhelming experiences and feelings resulting from trauma, and could be a vital tool for a young person's understanding of their own trauma responses.

Linda Hoggan, Psychotherapist and Co Director of Just What We Need Therapeutic Programme

This is an amazing book, written by a practitioner who clearly understands dissociation from the inside out.

It underlines the idea that it is equally important to be able to hold the negative feelings, as it is to show love and positivity, when working with/living with children and young people who have experienced trauma.

Jess really captures the essence of 'Dolly' within the story, and I am taken back to so many similar experiences of working with childhood trauma in my practice over the years – often with adults who rely on the 'baby Dolly' or 'Beastie' aspects of themselves when therapy feels too difficult.

I can see this book being used successfully with looked-after and adopted children in many settings. It is accessible to carers, practitioners and children themselves.

Thank you for writing it Jess, and for letting me read it.

Caroline Nicholas, Director, Langley Training

At last! A child-friendly, easy to read book (and workbook) about dissociation! Jess has yet again nailed it with her fourth book. Jess' ease of writing makes it easy for the reader to follow, young and old alike, explaining dissociation that everyone can understand through the words and beautiful illustrations which capture the fear and worries of the child and communicates exactly what is behind these big feelings.

This book is an utter joy to read and an absolute must for all children, parents, carers and professionals working within the trauma related field; fostering/adoption; looked-after children and also youth offending/criminal justice agencies. ***Beastie, Baby and The Brand-New Daddy*** outlines support strategies within the book that help our protagonist Dolly and her brand-new daddy. Jess has, yet again, ticked all of the boxes with her latest therapeutic workbook, it is a triumph! Not to be missed!

Carolyn Compston, Adolescent Practitioner

A thought-provoking book explaining dissociation in a straightforward, honest and relatable way. Jess has shared this successful method with our school, which we now use throughout our school.

Louise Day, Assistant Principal Robert Bloomfield Academy

Beastie, Baby and The Brand New Daddy

written by Jess van der Hoech
illustrated by Sophie Mikhailova

ISBN 978-1-8381987-4-9

Edited by Sarah Ogden
Illustrations by Sophie Mikhailova
Page layout design by Steve Mead Graphic Design

www.thegapbedfordshire.co.uk

For my son

Foreword

If I decided to buy a yellow car, it is almost guaranteed that the next time I went out driving, I would see yellow cars at every turn. Not because all of a sudden there was a surge in the number of purchases of yellow cars that were now on the road; they had always been there. The difference would be that I had now brought yellow cars into my awareness and would now notice them more. The same can be said for dissociation. When you know what it is you are looking for, your own perception changes. It is the moment you realise that these are not just the 'different feelings' that you've seen in a kids' movie or that you come to expect from being human. In its most extreme form, pathological dissociation is the process of a child taking on a completely different personality. Sometimes with a different voice, with a subtle difference in their facial expression, with an insistence that they ***hate*** sausages (which they've eaten a hundred times before with no issues), with a denial that it was their body that threw the object (which you have just seen them throw), the child that is described as being 'an absolute delight' by others who spend time with them and in ways that you just cannot recognise in the child that you spend time with yourself.

Dolly's story is one that I know well. Parenting a child who was so complex, so diverse in their behaviours; taking me on a daily journey of emotional rollercoasters, which at times left me wanting to shout 'Get me off! This is not what I signed up for!' while I fought the battle of wanting to be a good mum against admitting that my child and his behaviours were on the brink of defeating me. Fear of being judged for my own inadequacies as a parent left me scared to reach out for the help and support I desperately sought in caring for my child. When I did, I was very open about the fact that my child had lived the first two years of his life in circumstances of domestic violence and I was convinced that this was a contributing factor to the behaviours I was now seeing. When I left the specialist doctor, who had given him a diagnosis of Attention Deficit Hyperactive Disorder (ADHD), I breathed a sigh of relief. He had a chemical imbalance of his brain that could be treated with medication and I accepted that this was his diagnosis. Inherently, I knew that my child was traumatised from the violence he had witnessed in his early years. But with no professionals seeming to listen to me, the medical route felt like my only hope and so that was the path we followed.

After my son was diagnosed, I heard that there was no better person to be around a child with ADHD than one with counselling skills, so I attended night school to gain my diploma in therapeutic counselling. Part of my training involved me seeking my own personal therapy, during which my own trauma was fully processed. If it worked for me, surely it could also work for my child? The theory that he would not remember what had happened to him before the age of two had already been disproved on countless occasions when he re-enacted in exact sequence, some of the incidents he had witnessed. Determined to prove my own theory to myself, I embarked on a journey of learning about the impact of developmental trauma, where I was privileged enough to train with and learn from some of the most influential people in the therapeutic trauma world. That was when I discovered the term 'dissociation', and I realised that, unbeknown to me, the child I had been parenting had been dissociating and presenting with dissociative-self states for most of his life. I had seen multiple professionals, I had described these symptoms in detail to each and every one of them, but no one had ever said this word to me before. Moreover, no one had told me that by fully processing trauma through therapy, which could be done in a variety of modalities, the dissociative states could be integrated so he would become one cohesive, functioning 'self'. This is why Dolly's story, while simple, is effective. Because when you know what you're looking for, much like the yellow car, you begin to look for it, and if it is there - and only if it is there - you will recognise it.

How to use this book

First and foremost, ensure that both you and the child are well-regulated and comfortable when you begin to read Dolly's story. Make sure you choose a time when you are unlikely to be interrupted. The child may like a soother, a favourite or fidget toy, a drink or something to suck or chew to help them to stay regulated.

If the child is calm and begins to try and distract or move away from the reading, make a note of what they have just heard in the text. It is very likely that they will have just provided you with some valuable information about something that they cannot tolerate or want to avoid.

Dolly's brand-new daddy knows what to do and how to manage Beastie and Baby. If the child can relate to the story, it is important to assure them that sometimes being a 'brand-new daddy' can refer to learning a brand-new way of doing something, it does not mean that in order to be understood they need a different person to do the job alongside them.

Allow the child to notice the illustrations and see what they are able to identify with. The illustrations have been designed to give subtle suggestions to the child. For example, the chaotic streets of the houses which move into the more structured streets of Dolly's forever home and the appearance of Beastie beginning to soften towards the end as he is noticed and understood. Again, the illustrations can be very useful to open up and explore with the child what is going on in their internal world.

Examples of questions about the book

This list is not exhaustive by any means, but provides suggestions for conversation starters to help explore what is happening in the child's internal world. In the first instance, speak about Dolly and her 'inside team'; this removes the child from having to speak about themselves, which they might find difficult. It is likely that the child will give you their own information in the context of Dolly, which is more comfortable, being one step removed from them. Try not to correct the child about their interpretation of the story, simply do a lot of 'wondering' about what made them come to that conclusion.

- How do you think Dolly was feeling when she went to the new house?

- What might have stopped Dolly from telling the grown-ups about Beastie and Baby?
- How might Dolly feel when she knew her safe daddy understood about Beastie and Baby?
- Why do you think Dolly liked to hide?
- Is there anything else the daddy could have done that would help her to feel safe?
- How did Beastie feel when he came out?
- How did Beastie feel when he went back inside Dolly after he had been out?
- How did Dolly feel about what Beastie was doing?
- How did Baby feel when she came out?
- How did Baby feel when she went back inside Dolly after she had been out?
- How did Dolly feel about what Baby was doing?
- Could the safe daddy have done anything differently?
- What does 'safe' mean?
- What happened when Dolly did not feel safe?

There are a number of tools and techniques described in the book that help with emotional regulation and promote a sense of safety in the child's world. If a technique works well one day and not the next, have a think about which one of the inside team does not like that particular tool. It's also not uncommon for a child to resist something that is helping them. They have lived with their own very clever coping strategy in the form of self states, which may have gone completely unnoticed up until this point. You may have to explain the tools and techniques you have chosen to use several times; not all of the inside team come to listen to the same conversations at the same time and many will need to be repeated.

If you can find any therapeutic parenting resources in your area or online, this is a highly recommended approach to parenting a child who has experienced early trauma.

If you believe your child may be showing signs of dissociation, do not be afraid to ask for help and support.

Acknowledgments

To Dr Renee Marks, the first person I heard say the 'D' word in the keynote speech that took me on my journey into the world of dissociation. For the in-depth training, the knowledge and the passion you have in bringing this subject to the attention of the world, to change the lives of children, thank you.

With thanks to my trusted editor Sarah Ogden (Ogden Media), who seamlessly takes an ordinary document and turns it into a book. I know there is a lot of work that goes on behind the scenes that I remain completely oblivious to, choosing instead to believe that this whole process is entirely based on magic. Thank you.

To Sophie Mikhailova, who has interpreted what must have been the most bizarre job description into illustrations that have exceeded my expectations and gone beyond my wildest dreams. When the words are too much, the children will have the pictures, and these pictures really are quite special. Thank you.

To my wise, young friend (and his mum!) for all of the suggestions made throughout this process, which has contributed to this completed project. Your ideas were amazing. Thank you.

A very special thank you to my first born, who unknowingly gave me the most in-depth education about this subject and the courage to move forward with an unshakeable belief that the system can and should be changed, to help the millions of children who have learned to cope in their own special way.

About the author

Jess qualified as a Therapeutic Counsellor in 2014. She has experience working with high-risk adults and children who have witnessed or been subjected to extremely violent and complex situations and has focused her continuing professional development around the effects of trauma, with the impact of abuse becoming her specialist area. Jess has been trained to facilitate the ***Just What We Need*** therapeutic programme which was developed locally to support the emotional needs of parents and is now a national project. Most recently, Jess has founded The Gap (Bedfordshire) CIC; the first specialist therapeutic trauma provision for children in Bedfordshire. Jess is also the director of JV Trauma Tools and Training, which provides specialist training, products and ideas for anyone who is affected by the impact of trauma.

Beastie, Baby

and

The Brand New Daddy

Dolly sat in her new bedroom in her new house, looking at her new walls and her new furniture.
She breathed in, taking in the new smells and trying to work out if she liked them or not. Her ears picked up all the new sounds from outside. She could hear lots of birds singing. She had never lived in a house with so many birds singing outside and she wondered if she would ever get used to it.

Everything in Dolly's life was new.
She even had a new daddy.
The new daddy said this was going to be her 'forever home', but Dolly didn't really know what 'forever' meant.

Beastie street
2 year old street
birthday street
4.5 year old

You see, Dolly had already had four people doing the job of a daddy before this one. Whenever Dolly had a new daddy and a new home, things would always go wrong. All of the homes and all of the daddies had made different rules to follow and Dolly found it hard to know what she was supposed to do. She often found herself in trouble with the grown-ups around her.

When Dolly was very small, she had lived with a mummy and daddy who had given Dolly and her body very big hurts. The first mummy and daddy had not kept Dolly safe at all, so Dolly's brain had made a very clever plan.

Dolly had a Beastie who lived inside her. If Dolly ever thought that trouble or big hurts might happen, Beastie came to help her. The problem was, none of Dolly's daddies, teachers or any of the other grown-ups had known about Beastie, they thought it was Dolly who would shout or hit or do the things that Beastie did to protect Dolly.

Once, Dolly had been out shopping with one of the daddies in town and all of the noise and the strange people gave her a big, frightened feeling. Dolly often had frightened feelings and Beastie always came to help her. Beastie was big, strong and powerful and he could move super-quickly. Beastie took Dolly's body away from the frightened feeling as fast as he could, saving Dolly from the danger.

Suddenly Dolly felt a hand grab her arm. Beastie knew that Dolly didn't like her arm being grabbed, so with all his might, he turned and hit and kicked as hard as he could, while he shouted as loudly as he could! Big 'ROAAARRR's were coming from Dolly as Beastie saved her. But Beastie had been hitting and shouting at the person who was doing the job of the daddy at that time, and he was only trying to stop Dolly from running away and getting lost.

Sadly, Dolly got lots of frightened feelings and so Beastie had to come and protect her quite often. Because Beastie was the only one who had ever protected Dolly, she didn't want anyone to take him away from her, so she didn't tell anyone about Beastie and his important job.

When she was in trouble for something Beastie did, she would say "It wasn't me!" But nobody believed her.

When Dolly was in her own body, she was a lovely, kind, helpful eight-year-old girl. But nobody seemed to notice the good things about Dolly anymore, she always felt like she was in trouble.

Dolly really hoped that she could stay with this brand-new daddy, but she didn't really believe she would. Beastie would look after her though, of that she was certain.

Dolly had been staying with her new daddy for a few days and while she was learning about the new house and the new rules, Beastie had stayed hidden in her brain. One afternoon, Dolly was doing some writing with her new daddy. Very carefully, she tried to form all of her letters. Dolly found handwriting very tricky and she wished she could write neatly like the other children in her class at school. Dolly started to worry that the new daddy would say her handwriting was not good enough and she started to feel rubbish and useless.

"Don't worry!" said Beastie inside her head. "Just don't do it, let's do this instead!"

Beastie took Dolly's hand and scribbled hard over all of the work that Dolly had done so far. Beastie used Dolly's mouth to let out a big 'ROAAARRR' so the bad feeling could escape from Dolly's body.

Beastie looked at Dolly's new daddy who was sitting looking calmly at him.

"Hello there," he said. "I'm Dolly's safe daddy, what's your name?"

Beastie didn't know what to do. No one had ever spoken to him or asked his name before.

But Beastie wasn't going to be fooled.

He knew this was a grown-up who could give Dolly big hurts so with all his might he shouted, "I am Beastie and I hate everyone! Especially YOU!"

Beastie prepared for the brand-new daddy to shout back at him like the others used to, but instead he replied.

“It’s nice to meet you Beastie. I’m sorry you hate me, but I really like you. I wonder if I can get to know you just a little bit?”

Now Beastie was really confused.

“NO!” He roared. “No-one knows me! I look after Dolly!”

The brand-new daddy looked at Beastie thoughtfully. “I wonder, because it’s my job to look after Dolly and keep her safe, perhaps you could watch how I do that job for a while? Maybe then you might let me look after you too. What do you think?”

Beastie had never had a daddy look after him before, no one had ever looked after him at all. He had always looked after Dolly, ever since she was a baby. In fact, there was still a part of baby Dolly living inside her.

When Dolly had been a baby, she hadn't always been given the things she needed, like lovely warm milk in a bottle or nice baths with bubbles.

She had never had anyone to show her how to play with toys. Baby Dolly had always felt very sad about this and didn't want to grow up with so many sad feelings, so she had stayed as a baby.

next level

When baby Dolly had popped out before with the other mummies, they had told her to "Use your words," and "Stop being a baby!"

She couldn't stop being a baby though; she was a baby!

Beastie knew that this daddy would be the same, so he woke baby Dolly up inside, so he could prove that *he* should be the one to be in charge of looking after Dolly.

Baby Dolly woke up and eight-year-old Dolly's whole body slid off the chair and onto the floor underneath the table. Baby Dolly kicked the chair out of the way so she could stretch her legs out.

"Ga ga, goo goo goo," were the noises that started to come from Dolly's mouth.

The brand-new daddy came and crouched beside Dolly. "Hello little one, I'm your safe daddy. Do you want to come out here with me? I don't want you to hurt yourself on these chair legs.."

The new daddy started to move towards baby Dolly very carefully. He reached out and gently pulled baby Dolly onto his lap and gave her little kisses on her face. Baby Dolly liked that. The new daddy stroked her face. Baby Dolly liked that too.

“Would you like to play?” The new daddy asked as he carried Dolly into the living room and laid her gently on the floor. The new Daddy went and fetched a box from the cupboard under the stairs, it was full of baby toys. Baby Dolly was delighted. She had never seen so many toys before! She picked things up that twizzled and lit up.

She pressed buttons that made funny noises and animal sounds. Baby Dolly copied the noises. She found a rattle that made funny clicky sounds. The new daddy sat beside her, laughing and giggling with her and showing her how all of the toys worked.

When baby Dolly felt hungry, she let the new Daddy know by making crying sounds. The new daddy went to the kitchen and came back with a bottle of warm milk. She picked up baby Dolly and sat with her on the sofa while she drank her milk from the bottle. He made gentle 'cooing' sounds, telling Dolly how clever she was and asking her if her milk was nice.

Then he sang her a song. No one had ever sung a song to baby Dolly before and she loved it. It made her feel so relaxed that she began to fall into a peaceful sleep.

Eight-year-old Dolly came back into her own body. She looked at her new daddy and gave him a small smile. Dolly was starting to believe that it might be different with this new daddy, but she wasn't totally convinced.

Sometimes, when she got a big feeling, Dolly liked to hide under her blanket where nobody could see her. Dolly felt better for a while when she was under her blanket, but the grown-ups did not always like it when Dolly was hiding.

Sometimes, Dolly felt confused when she was under the blanket because as the big feelings started to go away, she couldn't remember which house she was in. This made Dolly feel scared to come out again.

The grown-ups thought Dolly was playing a game and pulled the blanket off her really quickly, sometimes shouting "BOO!" which gave Dolly's body a big shock!

Over the next few weeks, Dolly got to know the brand-new daddy more and more. The brand-new daddy spent every day teaching Dolly what 'safe' means. He explained that he was giving Dolly safe food, he held her hand as she crossed the road to keep her safe, he made sure Dolly had a bedtime to get all the sleep she needed because he was keeping her safe. Dolly's daddy wondered if being under her blanket made her feel 'safe' inside, which was why she liked being under there.

Dolly and the new daddy agreed that if Dolly was under the blanket, the new daddy would sing the same song each time she was there, so Dolly would know which house she was in and would not feel scared to come out from under the blanket. Dolly's new daddy put a pop-up tent in the corner of the living room, so if Dolly wanted to hide, she could go into her tent and peep out to check where she was. The new daddy promised that this would be Dolly's special place and he would never go into the tent unless Dolly invited her.

Dolly's new daddy put charts on the wall so that Dolly could always remember what she was supposed to do and could see what was going to happen at different times of the day. When Dolly went to school in the morning, she knew what was in her packed lunch and she knew what was going to be for dinner when she got home, so she never had to worry that she was going to be hungry.

At bath time, there were toys that baby Dolly could play with so she could have the lovely baths that she had missed out on. Every night, Dolly had a story and then baby Dolly had a bottle of warm milk and a song. If Beastie ever came to help, the new Daddy would always say "Hello Beastie! I see you're here, what do you need to tell me?"

The new daddy found out that Beastie liked to push really hard against a wall to help the big feelings to escape from Dolly's body. The new daddy would always tell Beastie how much he loved him.

Sometimes, Beastie would try very hard to get the new daddy to shout or be angry with him, but the new daddy kept telling him "I know you worked so hard for Dolly, but I can do this job now and I'd really like to be your daddy too."

One day the new daddy asked Beastie for a hug. Beastie had never had a hug before. He tried it and as he felt the new daddy's gentle arms around him, he thought how wonderful it felt to have a hug.

He didn't want the new daddy to think he wasn't big and powerful anymore so after the hug he shouted.

"Yuck! That was HORRID!"

but he knew the new daddy could tell he was smiling, just a little bit.

Kind words Garden
welcome
SAFETY
TRust

Dolly started to talk about the big hurts she had and the things that gave her the frightened and worried feelings. The new daddy helped Dolly to understand that the big hurts and the big feelings were not Dolly's fault. They worked out different ways that Dolly could make clever plans when she was in a tricky situation, so she could stay inside her own body and take charge.

The new daddy understood that Beastie and baby Dolly were wonderful and clever parts of Dolly and he wanted to be the daddy of all of the parts of her.

The new daddy was helping Dolly's brain to become stronger and every day he told Dolly lots of good words about herself. Dolly started saying them too. The more time the new daddy spent with baby Dolly, the more baby Dolly began to feel older, stronger and happier inside.

The safer Dolly felt every day, the stronger she felt inside and the eight-year-old Dolly spent more and more time in her own body. Baby Dolly grew so much that she became the same age as eight-year-old Dolly, but she stayed around to always remind Dolly how important it is to play and have fun.

Beastie decided that he could let this new daddy look after Dolly, but he would be in charge of helping Dolly to make the little plans she needed to help with any tricky days.

Dolly's brand-new daddy isn't her brand-new daddy anymore.

Now he is simply Dolly's Daddy.

By the same author

What A Muddle (2016) ISBN 978 18 38198 70 1

An interactive, practical workbook designed to help children who have difficulties with emotional regulation to begin to understand what is happening in their bodies. A variety of activities throughout the book enable the child to start to explore these ideas through the story of Sam, while gently encouraging them to begin to verbalise their own experiences. Carrying out the physical exercises in the book can promote changes in emotional regulation. The text is written in a child-friendly, gender-neutral style, and is easy to understand for parents, carers and practitioners alike. For children aged 4-12.

These Three Words (2018) ISBN 978 19 83047 57 2. Also available as an e-book.

A unique therapeutic novel for teenagers with the aim of linking together the feelings, emotions and behaviours connected to anxiety, with some of the therapeutic tools that can be used in order to enable better self-regulation, increased confidence and different ways of thinking. The book is equally valuable to parents of teenagers with anxiety, giving them an insight and understanding into some of the issues that may be affecting their child, and potentially opening up a line of communication and a way forward between parent and teen.

These Three Words: The Journal (2019) ISBN 978 18 38198 72 5

A thought-provoking and hands-on workbook, combining a series of practical exercises and tools designed to assist teenagers who are struggling with the symptoms of anxiety. Addressing the anxious responses in both brain and body, this journal provides the reader with the opportunity to discover therapeutic coping techniques and learn how to apply them to their own personal problem areas, before committing to a twenty-eight-day practice to promote good emotional regulation and reduced anxiety. The journal can be used alongside the therapeutic novel These Three Words, or as a standalone workbook, and it is suitable for use by the teenage reader on their own, with a parent, or in a group.

Printed in Great Britain
by Amazon

81954901R00038